SEEK

(Revised Edition)

Atchuthan Carvalho

Become Shakespeare.com

First published in 2018 by

Becomeshakespeare.com

Wordit Content Design & Editing Services Pvt Ltd
Unit - 26, Building A -1, Nr Wadala RTO,
Wadala (East), Mumbai 400037, India
T: +91 8080226699

Wordit Art Fund helps deserving authors publish
their work by providing monetary support.
To apply for funding, please visit us at
www.BecomeShakespeare.com

ISBN - 978-93-88081-75-7

Dedication

We are what we are taught to be and eventually as we grow up we start thinking for ourselves. What we are taught as a child has a lasting impression not just on our conscious way of thinking but most importantly our subconscious. The person I have become today would not have been possible if it wasn't for my mother's tireless efforts and belief in me. She somehow knew very well and believed so much that I am capable of more than what I thought of myself growing up. I had to go through a lot sour experiences and have a lot patience to truly understand what kind of a vision my Mom had for me.

During her time with me she was more than just my mother; she was my friend, my teacher and an awesome cook.

The day I had to bid her goodbye was the day I truly understood the meaning of unconditional love and what it really means to be a strong human being. I have also realized that strength is at times about learning to gracefully let go.

For her richness and wealth were always measured by values, beliefs and character and she left no stone unturned in living up to these principles herself.

I would like to dedicate this book to my mother Ms Flavia Carvalho. I pray she may know wherever she is how much I love her and miss her every day.

About the Author

 **Atchuthan Carvalho** is a post graduate in English literature from Mumbai University.

This book is a result of a search for a hidden truth in life which he has realised through his own research, meditation and reflection.

His quest had been to find out why humans suffer? Why there is so much pain in existence and why are some more happy than others!

After close to ten years of search and reflection, he has decided to share what he thinks through poetic verses.

Here he talks about Enlightenment and understanding the true nature of the world around us and knowing what's within.

Also follow him on

Facebook –
https://www.facebook.com/Atchuthanc/

LinkedIn -
https://www.linkedin.com/in/atchuthan-carvalho-14973512b

Instagram -
https://www.instagram.com/atchuthancarvalho

Acknowledgements

I would like to thank Leadstart and Wordit for helping me publish a revised edition of my book Seek. I was honestly caught by surprise as I was working on this already and their email dropped like a helping hand. It goes without saying that in such a competitive world it is undoubtedly difficult to publish, let alone be given an opportunity to rework and republish. Thank you whole heartedly.

A big thank you with love to my sister Marryliew Carvalho for her constant support and suggestions. Her relentlessness in "I got to take care of my big brother" attitude knows no bounds. She always has had a watchful eye on me and has always been eager to see me through my ambitions.

 I also thank my friend Yasmeen Shaikh for inspiring and being there for me whenever I have lost my way. Thank you for your time and effort in helping me pen and organise my thoughts for this book. I deeply thank you for your trust in me and my work.

Index

Introduction

Our minds are like fertile soil and we need to plant the seeds. In time, as the seed grows into a tree you too will grow in understanding the truth of life. I cannot promise you when and how you will understand, however do not chase the meaning. Let it dawn to you and always remember the following:

- ⊙ Use your intuition to feel your way.

- ⊙ Use your will power to walk that way.

- ⊙ Feel unconditional love in all that you face while you are on your way.

Realizing your true self and God is your destination. Self realization is the only goal worth striving for. You can know anything only as much as you know yourself. It is like the depth of the ocean; only as deep as you can imagine in your mind. The vastness of space is only as vast as you allow. The idea of God and Self also is as limiting as you allow it to be. The universe is not limited by what we believe, however we are limited by our own beliefs. Once we are able to break free from our own dogma of beliefs, can we begin to comprehend what reality really is. I have attempted to explain simple ideas of God, You (Self), Mind, Meditation and Will. The use of poetry I felt is more efficient at times; it helps getting you to the required feeling and understanding.

I encourage you to go through this book to make your own philosophy so that you can live your life to the fullest. Please do not drill any rules into your mind. Just remember, there is one eternal truth and you share a unique relation with this truth. Your place in this universe cannot be taken and this makes your understanding of the truth also unique.

Let's discern about God and You

The process to comprehend the due course of nature is not one to identify with the steps involved in it. In-fact, nature may not follow any predefined steps. Besides, the outcome of any situation is also significantly influenced by will power. Hence, if there are no fixed steps to understand nature and it becomes difficult to twig, then the change in perspective is imminent. We are currently looking at nature as an outward event happening independent of us. We need to realize that this is not the case and that nature works within us as much as out of us. More so within us and what we experience outside is a result of what we choose to manifest within.

This being understood, there is also another critical aspect of nature which we tend to overlook. We forget that she is alive and there is divinity in her ways. You as an individual have a purpose in accordance with this divine essence. You were sent here to experience that which you cannot experience in eternity. This may mean doing something either for others or maybe just for yourself. We have to align ourselves with this purpose; that can only happen when we align with our core nature and begin to be who we really are and feel like being.

Yes, death is certain and undeniably pain hurts, but have you wondered why we always want to experience new things and always seek something that makes us happy? It is because that's what we are here to do. Live, love, explore; be fearless while keeping in mind that you and your purpose are unique, so will be your path. Your obstacles will be as difficult as the strength of your will. God will not give you a problem that you cannot overcome; this would be against the entire purpose of creation. The possibility of reaching and completing your divine purpose because it is impossible for you to do is an impossible possibility. If there is a problem in your life and your heart tells you that you can solve it, then no matter how tough it may be, you have to succeed. Hence, it is very important to choose your path carefully and in accordance to this divine will and that can only be understood through prayers and faith. God may give you some ineffectual problems. Those are for you to just learn to fail and let go. It is to prepare you for what's next or even according to what is best for you now. Honestly, I cannot explain how the relationship that you share with divinity works for you. That's for you to find out. I promise you though that once you start being mindful, you will feel this connection with the divine and you will feel swayed.

'Enlightenment' is a word we have all heard and I am sure occasionally experienced as well. However, at times, we may not be able to decipher this word in its true sense, even though the gist of it may be right in front of us. With due course of time, however we are able to make sense out of this much presumed 'senseless experience'. Most importantly, there is no fundamental substantiation required once we know that we have attained the path of enlightenment. Basically we already know everything; it was just that one missing piece or spark which was vital for all of it to come together. What I have attempted in this collection of verses is to put together missing pieces or sparks which fit in our daily lives and will help us understand to a certain extent the true nature of things and our universe. Before you begin to read, there are a few things I would like to clarify. Whatever I have written are not rules to existence; in all honesty I believe that there are no rules to existence. Everything is the way it is made to be and can be made in an infinite number of ways.

There is a truth in this universe where we and everything comes from and will return to. This truth has been known by many names and will continue to be known by many names. This truth is infinite, omnipotent, omnipresent and omniscient. This truth is our very essence always was, is and will be. Since we are a part of this truth we have all of its qualities and hence each of us is as we wish to be. This truth has wished for the universe to be this way and similarly in some way or another we too have wished our lives to be this way.

Do not be too blissful about what you read or understand from what has been written here. You have to experience the truth for yourself and only then will it make a difference in your life.

What I have described here might have similarities with a lot of other philosophies that have been around for quite a long time. However I assure you that this similarity is not due to lack of ideas, but due to the very nature of truth.

The truth of our universe has never changed; the way we have described it always has. It is my pure intention that you learn to see this immortal truth. Do not be worried as you do not have to learn anything new. You are only in a process of realising what you already knew, but never realised. Enlightenment is all about realisation. This path does however require that we empty our mind of ego and accept that we do not know. An attitude of humble acceptance is always required so that we understand.

Verses:

1. What applies to one,
   Also applies to all.
   All of us are unique,
   And part of the same fall.

2. Wise words can be spoken by anyone,
   Without realizing they are wise.
   It is inherent in our very nature,
   The doubt is as we accept our disguise.

3. Being alone as it may be,
   Infinite creations though I see.
   I can have it all, I yet want more,
   Till I realize my soul, my shore.

4. Be true to yourself,
   And care not much,
   Your peace you deserve,
   And not what others say.
   Judge yourself, this truth shall remain,
   You will find peace in your way.

5. Love not with a petite heart,
   Love is easy, love is instinctive.
   What makes it impure is attachment,
   Hence gets stale and thus defective.

6. Darkness exhibits the absence of light,
    Hatred demonstrates the absence of love.
    Hunger intends the absence of food,
    Sadness in life is due to the absence of good.

7. I pray to thee,
    For strength to be.
    I know the truth I know,
     And will not stop till the truth I be.

8. Be not afraid of failures,
    Replace that thought with faith.
    Strength that you get from within,
    Shall forgive even the devil's mistake.

9. Fall and fall, to rise and rise.
    Keep the strength, if ahead failure lies.
    Nothing is absolute even when it seems,
    Only once you give up, you lose all things.

10. Nature might appear in chaos,
    Everything living to die is seen,
    But what is seen is only a glimpse,
    For he who knows the master within.

11. Wise words are spoken by many,
    But (space) are understood by a few.
    Wisdom we presume is taught to us,
    While this is quite far from true.
    Already she resides, within you and me alike.
    Find the way and she will eagerly make you bright.

12. The world spins due to the art of balance,
    If something is taken then is surely replaced.
    Your life too is a similar art,
    Balance well or be spun out of place.

13. Which is the right way and which is not,
    A doubt already our minds have got.
    Nature has made all from her,
    The path you choose also by her.
    If one claims to explain her infinite glory,
    Then I will be the first to doubt that story.

14. God is not a high heaven up above,
    Up is empty space and stardust.
    Even if God exits somewhere up there,
    The way is still felt in our heart's despair.

15. I am trying to explain,
    The truth hidden in plain
    Must you believe and feel it exists,
    And then see the bliss.

16. Don't doubt your path one bit,
    Know so well in every heart beat.
    Every soul's destiny in the universe is one.
    Question here is when that moment shall come.

17. Tough it is to explain that feeling within,
    It reminds that not all I have seen.
    I was born and then learnt that I am lost,
    Only to find again, that I am the cause of all cause.

18. It is right here and now,
    Right in front of your eyes somehow.
    You don't need an instrument to tell you how it feels,
    Its alive in your heart if you may listen to it please.

19. In a night of flawless beauty,
    The moon shines in all its grace.
    Apparently appears so rough and rugged,
    Yet so sublime, devoid of a mistake.

20. Both good and evil are here to stay,
    God has made our world that way.
    Light cannot shine,
    Unless darkness darkens with might.
    One wins and then the other,
    Like in a dance they are bind (bound) together.

21. Have faith in you and believe without doubt,
    Know in your heart what you truly scout,
    At the end be it for better or worse,
    God knows what you have and what you deserve.

22. At times when only obstacles we find,
    Steady your faith and know God is kind,
    Where god wishes you to be is the essence of freedom,
    He may have tied you down in chains,
    Testing you to devotedly trust his wisdom.

23. Always smile and be playful,
    Always know your centred self.
    Know what god wants is best for you,
    Even if that means changing yourself too.

Verses:

24. It's a short life through many a year,
    An eternal truth awaits us here,
    You were born to live a fulfilling dream.
    But how can this be done,
    Without the truth being seen.

25. Know what you seek,
    Seek and you shall find,
    When you find you would know,
    The universe is pleasant and kind.

26. We see others in pain,
    Mostly it makes us weep,
    Try not worrying about this though,
    God's justice is true and deep.

27. Some say you dwell in the heart,
    Some say you dwell beyond us all,
    Some say you are in heaven,
    Then you say, "I right you all".

28. Look deep within,
    Look deep (space) at what's out,
    What you find in the end,
    Is the same throughout.

29. Death is a fear we all possess,
    And a fact we all shall face,
    But since death is my absence,
    Death shall find me difficult to trace.

30. A sadness that fills the heart,
     A happiness it longs to find,
     What do I do to get in there?
     To find solace from this despair.

31. Dig deep into your heart with prayer.
    Know that what you see is not all of it,
    Dig even deep into yourself,
    Know that what you think is not all of it.

32. Don't chase the world too much,
    It does whatever it wants you see,
    Live life as per your pace,
    And you too will find your destiny.

33. I seek you here,
    I seek you there,
    I am so glad to find,
    That thou art everywhere.

34. Look for the signs of God,
    Listen to the music that calls,
    Nature always talks to us all,
    Blind and dumb she loves us all.

35. Make it worthwhile,
    Every second that we spend,
    We don't have to worry,
    Everything is alright in the end.

36. The sky stretches so far,
      We can see God even there,
      Infinite is what describes Him best,
      But only through you can he be everywhere.

37. We have a path which we all walk,
      Sometimes with others or alone maybe,
      In truth we are always alone,
      So cherish with love what each moment be.

38. Nothing is not nothing,
      Like a blank sheet is not nothing,
      Nothing is the truth to all,
      Like a womb to everything.

39. His name is that,
      What all call all,
      It is only he who knows,
      Yesterday tomorrow and all.

40. I have a certain hope for you,
      I am very sure that you already knew,
      To find again where you come from,
      To teach yourself that only you can accrue.

41. Seek wisdom always,
      The rest is always there,
      Find the truth in all,
      A happy life does wisdom bear.

42. There is an essence in all,
    And all are in this essence,
    Like the one power that runs,
    To play life in playful ways.

43. When light glows in the dark,
    The darkness turns to light,
    Every good deed done in life,
    Makes our soul mighty bright.

44. Don't give up on this long road,
    Obstacles are the bricks of life,
    Don't give up on yourself either,
    As you are, the essence of life.

45. Man tries to make sense of the universe,
    Senseless indeed is man,
    Why should there be sense in the universe,
    When she is in every way she can.

46. Light of truth is always bright,
    Always was, is, and will be,
    It exists without cause,
    Hence is at times difficult to see.

47. Omnipotent Omnipresent Omniscient,
    This might describe the truth somewhat,
    But why do we have to search for it,
    When this is what everything one has got.

Meditation, Mind and Will

The idea of the mind is usually associated with thoughts and that surprisingly is just one aspect of it. The mind involves not just our thoughts but also our feelings, memory, imagination, intuition, will power and many other aspects of our being. It is safe to boldly state that the mind is everything and if it is not in our mind then I doubt if it can be anywhere else. Any aspect of experience about us starts and ends finally in the human mind. The mind is the only one thing that really matters and is always free of bondage and surroundings. The only challenge being weather you allow your mind to be so or not.

The mind is yours and in all honesty does whatever you allow it to. Whatever you give or have given attention to thrives in the mind. If your mind is free of a particular idea, for example a feeling of fear, then no matter how real that particular fear maybe you will not be affected by it.

The mind truly encompasses the idea of freedom. A free mind creates the true essence of freedom.

To put this more into perspective, think of yourself as an awareness or consciousness. Now you have a mind which is the first aspect of your being. Everything that you are and want to be or are destined to be passes through the mind from your eternal consciousness before becoming a reality.

The mind is your tool for eternal creation and there are many attainments or abilities to this tool.

The ultimate attainment is God or self realization where you realize that you are the same as universal consciousness.

This topic of the mind has many aspects and explaining them all is next to impossible. However, what I have mentioned should be good enough for you to detach yourself from the mind and know that you are separate from it. Your mind is your creation and always will be what you choose to create in it. Others may influence it however that completely depends on how much you allow it.

All that has ever been taught and will ever be taught is ultimately just a way to free yourself from of your mind and the thoughts arising in your mind. No one can explain God and reality. God has to be experienced. The only one way for you to know the truth is for you to see it for yourself and this can never be done with a niggling mind.

Now in order to understand our mind, we need to observe and study it. This is a journey where you have to be your own teacher. I shall use the term meditation however meditation is not a physical act. It is you separating yourself from your thoughts by being silent in your own mind. It is a practice of detachment from emotions, habits and impulses. Meditation is never about stopping or controlling the thoughts and feelings. It is the ability to see everything as it is and not be affected by it. All this is within you. Once you are able to achieve this state, you your self will be able to understand which thoughts or feelings have what meaning. The real you will be discernible and so will be your real strengths and weakness.

All this is easier said than done and is just like any other aim in life. There will be ups and downs. There will be confusions and distractions. There will not be any measurable results. There will just be you and your mind. However I guarantee you that this journey will free you and this journey is what real freedom is. Unless and until we do not understand our own mind then it does not matter which part of the universe we are in, a weak mind will always yield a weak life and strong mind a strong life.

Now we need to decide to be strong internally and one of our most helpful abilities is will power. It is only by will can we pass through the unforgiving failures and obstacles of not just our mind but also our lives.

By willpower, I do not mean a fighting attitude of a war cry. I mean a silent, steady, quite, flexible mindset, that which is willing to take the hits and get back up, that is willing to walk the path as destined. A willpower that is strong enough to let go of what is dearest to you and yet love unconditionally. Will is by far one of the most important tool while we start of on this journey within our own self. Once we have made up our mind that we want to know our real self then true failure will only happen if you give up on this path. If you do not give up ever then success is yours for sure.

Verses:

1. What we seek we always find,
   Don't doubt this way and be blind.
   We everyday chase what we cannot see,
   Unless we doubt it and it ceases to be.

2. It shall come for sure,
   We have to wait though till it's here.
   Never doubt that you will be redeemed,
   Smile already and your manifestation will be seen.

3. Moving mountains is easy,
   Unless the thought of it seems heavy.
   Through thoughts the world is divided,
   Through thoughts alone our fate is decided.

4. A lonely soul walks a lonesome path,
   Seeking happiness along its path.
   We have forgotten that within the truth is still,
   True bliss is our creation and in will.

5. Thought is a tricky thing,
   Its absence is not a thinking thing.
   Freedom from thoughts is a thoughtful way,
   But this blissful truth is not in the thinking way.

6. We cannot see without our eyes,
    We cannot hear without our ears.
    We cannot do anything without the mind,
    But beyond the mind resides something divine.

7. You will know how to get there,
    Even while you are on your way.
    It is like your heart will tell you,
    I know what I am doing so just walk this way.

8. Our worries of tomorrow,
    Are the reasons of our pain.
    Pain that is yet to arrive later,
    Makes our present pretty insane.
    Here and now is all there is,
    Rest are mere overwhelming mental worries.

9. God's precision is prefect as they say,
    He has made us all in his own way.
    An infinite part is infinite still,
    Filling this with doubt is all **at (remove)** your will.

10. We need to know that we cannot stop,
    Strive on with diligence to the enlightened spot.
    We once chose to come from our grace divine.
    To live on the earth and practice this kind.
    But we have forgotten our grace in doubtful ways,
    By choice and by will can we recover our grace.

11. Meditation for us is a thoughtful thing,
     We use thoughts even to dance and sing.
     Without the thinking when dancing is done,
     And beyond thinking meditation is sung.
     A presence is known that is not a thought,
     Reaching here is what we all should have sought.

12. Imagine how creation has made all there is,
     Wonder how the universe works.
     Is it in God's mind where rules are made,
     Just as he has willed we have all obeyed.

13. Seek it here,
     Seek it now,
     Yesterday and tomorrow,
     Are never yours somehow.
     Wherever you are,
     Right now is the time,
     Just breathe and believe,
     That now is always mine.

14. We seek a life eternal,
     We seek a path that will lead.
     Blinded we are in earthly ways,
     As eternal life is in heavenly deeds.

15. What is appropriate, what is not,
     Being normal is what everyone has got.
     It is hilarious, if one can see,
     Nothing nowhere is normal.
     Everything living and dying to be.

16. How we accept our world,
    Is based on what is around.
    If it were filled with flying humans,
    Nobody would find it profound.

17. The greatest test is waiting,
    Patience is all it takes.
    Your destiny comes towards you,
    Chasing it is a big mistake.

18. One needs to know,
    That one may not always know.
    When it is time it is time,
    Everything eventually has got to go.

19. Wave after wave,
    Is what makes the ocean rough.
    Thought after thought,
    Is what makes clarity tough.
    Steady the mind one wave at a time,
    Still the ocean, bottom you will find.

20. Learning means to accept,
    That you don't know and shall embrace.
    For something wise to find its way,
    Silence the mind hence wisdom may say.

21. Beauty is ugly,
    Ugly is beautiful.
    They both make each other seen.
    How would you know what's what,
    Unless a comparison has been seen.

22. This dance is one between two extremes,
     Happy and sad, good and bad.
     The idea is to sway and do so well,
     A steady mind can dance this well.

23. The ideal way is both,
     Proactive or reactive thinking is fine.
     Being thoughtless is an art in existence,
     When we know an empty mind is also fine.

24. Do not desire as it hurts you know,
     Do not want anything to live happily even more,
     If these lines are truly desire free,
     Read them again and again till the truth you see.

25. This game is all about memory,
     Forgotten we have our true identity.
     We see in a mirror and assume we are that,
     Not really seeing our temporary act.
     Meditation will show us a reflection too,
     There you will see the eternal you.

26. I prefer to write but little,
     Cause it's best for you to see,
     My intent is only to guide you through,
     It's up to you where you want to be.

27. Don't doubt the emptiness within,
     Even though you may fill it with everything,
     Whatever is born will one day die,
     Everlasting emptiness is not a lie.

28. We all have a home in this universe,
     Free from rent and bills,
     We come from there to rent in this world,
     Eventually though we will gain back our still.

29. We doubt the truth every day,
     But seldom do we doubt this way,
     Never do we sit and see,
     The thoughts we think and then doubt to be.

30. I looked once,
     Then I looked again,
     I still kept looking,
     Yet I couldn't see everything.

31. Look not that far,
     For what you have not,
     You may get it all,
     And still doubt what you got.

32. Have no doubt in your heart,
     Doubt will always come and scare,
     Even when you have faith in your heart,
     Doubt will still come and try to scare.

33. Why do we do what we do?
     Why do we not stop to find?
     Why do we not worry of what draws us?
     What are we so afraid to find?

34. Endlessly stretched beyond end,
    The mind's thought cannot bend,
    Thoughts finite cannot see beyond,
    Like one cannot see the sky's end.

35. There is no mystery in the universe,
    There is only mystery in the universe,
    Both are just two sides,
    All due to our ignorant minds.

36. Let it all flow,
    Let your heart know,
    Everything causes everything,
    Together only can souls grow.

37. Empty your mind,
    Difficult it is indeed,
    It is like thinking to think not,
    But maybe someday we will all succeed.

38. We are free in every way,
    Even free to doubt this way,
    Nothing can hold us down,
    Unless we choose to live that way.

39. Do not worry about it,
    Worrying is a waste of time,
    Do not be too happy about it,
    That too is a waste of time.

40. I can write anything,
     Not worrying what it means,
     Our minds are made to make sense,
     After seeing chaos in all things.

41. Learning never stops,
     After a lot there is a lot more,
     Knowing never stops too,
     But after a lot there is no more.

42. These lines come from within one's self,
     Nothing too fancy just being one's self,
     All of us have this in us,
     To find it though, we shall look for it first.

43. Meditation is like a level's jump,
     But jumping will not get you there,
     It's like a thoughtful wish,
     But thinking will not get you there.

44. Lost are most of us,
     And most of us don't know,
     To know being lost is a blessing,
     And when you know then trust the flow.

45. It makes us wonder,
     What tomorrow brings,
     All we have is now,
     As yesterday and tomorrow are barmy things.

46. New things smile when they come,
    Old things cry when they go,
    This is how it will always be,
    We need to learn to accept the show.

47. We enjoy peace,
    We enjoy happiness,
    Wonder if we enjoy to experience,
    Even war and sadness.

Conclusion

We have a path to choose; this path is our ultimate one. This way is within and leads to the source that created everything. This way is unique to all of us as each of us is unique. We may never know for sure what our path is till we listen our own calling. If we pay attention to that, we will know which way we are meant to walk and what decisions we are suppose to take. We will not be fearful or confused in uncertainty and will be able to live a more fulfilling life in accordance with the divine.

Understanding ourselves as creators of our destiny in accordance with our divine purpose is the ultimate way to realize our true potential. We need to know deep down what we are meant to do and then choose the door through which we want to walk through. We cannot make such decisions or take a risk unless and until we understand our own self and our own mind.

Nature will always give you signs and signals, however will always leave the ultimate choice to you. If you are with a weak mind and not well grounded in yourself then you will be hesitant to change yourself and hence change your life. Just like how I have tried my best to give you a version of reality which can change the course of your life. However, at the end the ultimate choice is yours. A door remains open for a certain period of time in life so when it is time to choose don't hesitate even if the ambiguity scares you. As long as your heart knows deep down that this is where your calling is, just surrender to the tide and go with the flow. This, at times may not be in sync with your logic and reasoning but you will know deep down whom you should trust.

Again, all this is only possible if we are attuned to God, to ourselves and to our mind. I know you shall realize very well deep down the message of this book. You will not be able to be happy in life unless and until you seek the truth and the way to the truth is beyond the peripheries of our mind. Hence, choose today to make a difference in your own mind for your own self. Choose to be happy and peaceful. Listen to what God has in store for you and beware of the signs God gives. He will not force a way on you because he expects us to become wiser with the choices that we make. He will let you be stupid or wise and let karma take its course.

All that is written here are just ways to free your mind. Please do not assume these to be right or wrong unless and until it makes sense to you. Encourage yourself to learn more about yourself. Know that the outside world cannot ever be changed. The only change is that which comes from within. The only real power is that of your own mind. The only real saviour is your own self. Realization of your dormant potential will lead to extra ordinary things in your own life. Once you are able to change yourself for the better and feel better by yourself, then you would truly be able to make a difference in the lives of your own families and the greater world around.

Start to sit and seek to be,

Reflect within and the truth you'll see.

For your journey to begin your choice is first,

Your heart will beat for the choice you must.

www.ingramcontent.com/pod-product-compliance
Lightning Source LLC
Chambersburg PA
CBHW051407130726
47987CB00007B/2888